DED...

EASY
ITALIAN
PHRASE BOOK FOR
TRAVEL

Easy Italian Phrase Book for Travel
Over 1200 words for every situation, from common
expressions to slang, and even unique phrases to stand out

Made by Journey Joy
Designed by Giorgia Ragona

www.agenziadedalo.it

Index

Introduction

Welcome to your new adventure in Italy! Whether you're planning a dream vacation, a quick getaway, or even considering a longer stay in the land of pasta and sunshine, this little book is your trusty travel buddy. Learning a new language can be intimidating, but don't worry—we're keeping things light, fun, and, most importantly, easy. No complicated grammar rules or endless vocabulary lists here—just the phrases you need to get by, make friends, and enjoy every moment of your Italian experience.

Purpose of the Phrase Book

This phrasebook is designed to be your go-to resource for all things Italian while you're traveling. We've stripped away the unnecessary complexities and focused on what you really need: practical phrases that will help you navigate everyday situations with ease. Whether you're ordering a cappuccino, buying train tickets, or simply making small talk, the goal is to equip you with the language tools to make your trip smooth, enjoyable, and full of memorable moments.

Think of this book as your pocket-sized passport to better experiences. With just a few phrases, you can turn a simple interaction into a delightful exchange, making your journey more immersive and, dare we say, a bit more magical.

How to Use This Book

Using this phrasebook is as simple as flipping to the section you need and finding the right phrase for the moment. We've organized everything by theme—like eating out, shopping, and getting around—so you can quickly find what you're looking for without having to wade through pages of unrelated content.

Each phrase comes with an easy-to-understand pronunciation guide, so you'll sound as close to a local as possible, even if you're just starting out.

Don't worry if you don't have time to memorize phrases before your trip. This book is designed for on-the-go use. The book's pocket size means you can carry it with you wherever you go—no Wi-Fi or data needed!

Basic Pronunciation Guide

Italian pronunciation is actually quite straightforward, especially for English speakers. The good news is that Italian words are generally pronounced the way they are spelled. This section will give you a quick rundown on how to make your Italian sound as smooth as possible, so you can order that perfect espresso without a hitch.

Here's a little secret: in Italian, every letter has a voice. Unlike English, where some letters like to stay silent (we're looking at you, "k" in "knight"), in Italian, you pronounce everything you see. Vowels are consistent, too. "A" is always like "ah," "E" like "eh," and so on. Once you get the hang of these basics, you'll find that reading and pronouncing Italian words is a breeze.

Note that the pronunciation guides you'll find in parentheses aren't based on phonetic rules—they're designed to be simple, intuitive, and easy to follow. We've taken a more informal approach to help you get a feel for how the words sound without any complications. So don't worry about perfection or technicalities; the goal is to make sure you're understood and to help you enjoy your Italian experience without any stress!

Tips for Effective Communication in Italy

One of the best tips we can give you is to start your interactions in Italian, even if it's just a simple "Ciao!" or "Buongiorno!" This shows respect for the local culture and often results in a warmer reception. Even if the conversation switches to English later, starting off in Italian sets a friendly tone.

Enjoy the adventure!

CHAPTER 1

Essential Italian Phrases

Welcome to the heart of your Italian adventure—learning the essential phrases that will make your trip smooth, fun, and full of delightful interactions. Whether you're strolling through ancient streets, dining in a cozy trattoria, or simply asking for directions, these handy phrases will be your best friends. They're easy to learn, easy to use, and will help you navigate the everyday moments that make traveling so special.

Greetings and Polite Expressions

In Italy, greetings are more than just words—they're a way of showing respect and warmth. Whether you're meeting someone for the first time or bumping into a friend, knowing how to greet people properly will make you an instant favorite!

- **Ciao!** (chow) – *Hi! / Bye!*
  Perfect for informal situations, this versatile word works both when you're saying hello and when you're heading out. It's like the Italian version of "Aloha"!
- **Buongiorno!** (bwohn-jor-noh) – *Good morning!*
  Start your day with a cheerful "Buongiorno!" It's polite and works anytime from dawn until around 4 PM.
- **Buonasera!** (bwohn-ah-seh-rah) – *Good evening!*
  Switch to "Buonasera" in the late afternoon and evening. It's a great way to greet someone at dinner or when you're out for an evening stroll.
- **Arrivederci!** (ah-ree-veh-der-chee) – *Goodbye!*
  The formal way to say goodbye. Use this when leaving a shop or after a polite conversation.
- **Per favore** (pehr fah-voh-reh) – *Please*
  Politeness counts! Add this to any request, and you're sure to get a smile.
- **Grazie!** (grah-tsyeh) – *Thank you!*
  You'll be using this one a lot. Don't forget to say "Grazie" after receiving your gelato or directions!
- **Prego!** (preh-goh) – *You're welcome!*
  A lovely little word that means you're welcome. You might hear it often after saying "Grazie."
- **Mi scusi** (mee skoo-zee) – *Excuse me*
  Whether you're trying to get someone's attention or squeezing past in a crowded piazza, this phrase is your go-to.

These phrases will help you start on the right foot with everyone you meet. Italians appreciate when visitors make an effort, so don't be shy—start every interaction with a smile and one of these greetings!

Common Questions and Responses

Getting around Italy is a lot easier when you know how to ask the right questions—and understand the answers! Here are some handy phrases to keep conversations flowing smoothly.

- **Dove si trova...?** (doh-veh see troh-vah) – *Where is...?*
  Use this to ask for directions. Just fill in the blank: *Dove si trova il bagno?* (Where is the bathroom?)
- **Quanto costa?** (kwahn-toh koh-stah) – *How much does it cost?*
  A must-know when shopping. Whether you're eyeing a souvenir or a scoop of gelato, this phrase will come in handy.
- **Parla inglese?** (par-lah een-gleh-zeh) – *Do you speak English?*
  In case you need to switch to English, this is a polite way to ask if someone can understand you.
- **Che ore sono?** (keh oh-reh soh-noh) – *What time is it?*
  Lost track of time while wandering through ancient ruins? No worries—just ask!
- **Posso avere...?** (pohs-soh ah-veh-reh) – *Can I have...?*
  Perfect for ordering in restaurants or asking for something in a store: *Posso avere un caffè?* (Can I have a coffee?)
- **Dov'è il bagno?** (doh-veh eel bah-nyoh) – *Where is the bathroom?*
  Trust me, you'll want to remember this one!
- **Può aiutarmi?** (pwoh ah-yoo-tar-mee) – *Can you help me?*
  If you're feeling stuck or confused, this phrase is your lifeline.

With these questions and responses, you'll be ready to navigate most situations with ease. And remember, Italians are generally friendly and willing to help—especially if you start the conversation in their language!

Numbers, Days, and Time

Understanding the basics of numbers, days, and time will make your Italian adventure run more smoothly. Let's dive into the essentials that will help you keep track of your trip and avoid any scheduling mix-ups!

Numbers:

- **Uno** (oo-noh) – *One*
- **Due** (doo-eh) – *Two*
- **Tre** (treh) – *Three*
- **Quattro** (kwah-troh) – *Four*
- **Cinque** (cheen-kweh) – *Five*
- **Sei** (say) – *Six*
- **Sette** (seh-teh) – *Seven*
- **Otto** (oht-toh) – *Eight*
- **Nove** (noh-veh) – *Nine*
- **Dieci** (dyeh-chee) – *Ten*

Once you've got these down, combining them is easy! For example, **venti** (twenty) + **due** (two) = **ventidue** (twenty-two). Math has never been this much fun!

Days of the Week:

- **Lunedì** (loo-neh-dee) – *Monday*
- **Martedì** (mar-teh-dee) – *Tuesday*
- **Mercoledì** (mehr-koh-leh-dee) – *Wednesday*
- **Giovedì** (joh-veh-dee) – *Thursday*
- **Venerdì** (veh-nehr-dee) – *Friday*
- **Sabato** (sah-bah-toh) – *Saturday*
- **Domenica** (doh-meh-nee-kah) – *Sunday*

Days of the week are straightforward, but keep in mind that many businesses close on **Domenica**. Use this list to plan your adventures wisely!

Telling Time:

- **Che ore sono?** (keh oh-reh soh-noh) – *What time is it?*
- **È l'una.** (eh loo-nah) – *It's one o'clock.*

- **Sono le due.** (soh-noh leh doo-eh) – *It's two o'clock.*
- **Mezzogiorno** (med-zoh-jor-noh) – *Noon*
- **Mezzanotte** (med-zah-noh-teh) – *Midnight*
- **E mezza** (eh med-zah) – *and a half* (as in 2:30)
- **E un quarto** (eh oon kwahr-toh) – *and a quarter* (as in 3:15)

These time phrases will help you make sure you're never late for that delicious dinner reservation. Italians love to enjoy their meals, and so should you—on time!

With these essential phrases under your belt, you're all set to start your Italian journey with confidence and a smile. Whether you're saying "Buongiorno!" to a new friend or figuring out how much that beautiful leather bag costs, you'll be ready for anything. Buon viaggio!

CHAPTER 2

Travel and Transportation

Navigating Italy is part of the adventure! Whether you're hopping on a bus, renting a car for a scenic drive, or finding your way through a bustling airport, these phrases will help you get from point A to point B with ease—and maybe even a little bit of flair. Let's make sure you're not just getting around, but doing it like a local!

Asking for Directions

Finding your way in Italy is all part of the charm, but when Google Maps just isn't cutting it, these phrases will help you ask for directions (and understand the answers!).

- **Dove si trova...?** (doh-veh see troh-vah) – *Where is...?*
  Fill in the blank with your destination: *Dove si trova il Colosseo?* (Where is the Colosseum?)
- **Come si arriva a...?** (koh-meh see ah-ree-vah ah) – *How do you get to...?*
  Perfect for asking for walking or driving directions: *Come si arriva al centro storico?* (How do you get to the historic center?)
- **È lontano?** (eh lon-tah-noh) – *Is it far?*
  Useful for gauging whether you need to walk, take a bus, or grab a taxi.
- **A destra** (ah deh-strah) – *To the right*
  A sinistra (ah see-nees-trah) – *To the left*
  Dritto (dree-toh) – *Straight ahead*
  Basic direction words to help you follow instructions.
- **Vicino** (vee-chee-noh) – *Nearby*
  Lontano (lon-tah-noh) – *Far away*
  These will help you understand just how close—or far—your destination is.

Don't be afraid to ask for directions—Italians are usually happy to help, and you might even discover a hidden gem along the way!

Using Public Transport

(Bus, Train, Taxi)

Public transport in Italy is generally efficient and easy to use, but knowing a few key phrases can make the experience smoother and more enjoyable.

- **Dove prendo l'autobus?** (doh-veh pren-doh low-too-boos) – *Where do I catch the bus?*
  Handy when you're looking for the nearest bus stop.
- **Un biglietto per favore.** (oon beel-lyet-toh pehr fah-voh-reh) – *One ticket, please.*
  Whether you're on a bus, train, or tram, you'll need this phrase to get your ticket.
- **Quanto costa il biglietto?** (kwan-toh koh-stah eel beel-lyet-toh) – *How much is the ticket?*
  Make sure you have the right change or your card ready!
- **A che ora parte il prossimo treno?** (ah keh oh-rah par-teh eel prohs-see-moh treh-noh) – *What time does the next train leave?*
  Perfect for planning your journey.
- **Dov'è la stazione?** (doh-veh lah stah-tsee-oh-neh) – *Where is the station?*
  Use this when you're looking for the train or bus station.
- **Mi porta a...?** (mee por-tah ah) – *Can you take me to...?*
  Essential for taxi rides: *Mi porta a Piazza Navona?* (Can you take me to Piazza Navona?)
- **Può fermarsi qui, per favore?** (pwoh fehr-mar-see kwee pehr fah-voh-reh) – *Can you stop here, please?*
  Useful in a taxi or bus when you've reached your destination.

Using public transport is a great way to see the sights and get a feel for local life. Plus, it's a lot of fun—especially when you've got the right phrases at your fingertips!

Renting a Car

Ready to hit the road? Renting a car gives you the freedom to explore Italy at your own pace. Here's how to navigate the rental process and beyond.

▸ **Vorrei noleggiare un'auto.** (vor-ray noh-lej-jah-reh oon ow-toh) – *I'd like to rent a car.*
Start off by letting them know what you need.

▸ **Quanto costa al giorno?** (kwan-toh koh-stah ahl jor-noh) – *How much does it cost per day?*
This is important for budgeting your road trip.

▸ **È compresa l'assicurazione?** (eh kohm-preh-zah lah-see-koo-rah-tsee-oh-neh) – *Is insurance included?*
Always check what's covered in the rental agreement.

▸ **C'è il navigatore satellitare?** (cheh eel nah-vee-gah-toh-reh sah-teh-lee-tah-reh) – *Is there a GPS?*
Unless you want to rely on your phone or old-school maps, this could be a lifesaver.

▸ **Dov'è il distributore di benzina più vicino?** (doh-veh eel dee-stree-boo-toh-reh dee ben-tzee-nah pyoo vee-chee-noh) – *Where is the nearest gas station?*
A must-know when your tank starts to run low!

▸ **Posso avere una mappa?** (pohs-soh ah-veh-reh oo-nah mahp-pah) – *Can I have a map?*
Just in case you prefer paper to pixels for navigating.

With these phrases, you'll be ready to explore the Italian countryside, discover charming small towns, and maybe even stumble upon a hidden beach. Buckle up and enjoy the ride!

At the Airport

Whether you're arriving in or departing from Italy, knowing what to say at the airport can make your journey much smoother. Here's how to handle check-ins, security, and finding your way around.

▶ **Dove si trova il check-in?** (doh-veh see troh-vah eel check-in) – *Where is the check-in?*
Perfect for when you first enter the airport.

▶ **Ho una prenotazione.** (oh oo-nah preh-noh-tah-tsee-oh-neh) – *I have a reservation.*
Use this when you're checking in your flight.

▶ **Posso avere il mio biglietto?** (pohs-soh ah-veh-reh eel mee-oh beel-lyet-toh) – *Can I have my ticket?*
Handy if you're picking up your ticket at the counter.

▶ **Dove sono i controlli di sicurezza?** (doh-veh soh-noh ee kon-troll-lee dee see-kyoor-eh-tzah) – *Where is security?*
Important for finding your way to the security checks.

▶ **Qual è il numero del mio gate?** (kwahl eh eel noo-meh-roh del mee-oh gate) – *What is my gate number?*
Don't miss your flight—make sure you're at the right gate.

▶ **A che ora parte l'aereo?** (ah keh oh-rah par-teh lah-eh-reh-oh) – *What time does the plane leave?*
Good to know, especially if you're waiting in the lounge.

▶ **Dove posso ritirare i bagagli?** (doh-veh pohs-soh ree-tee-rah-reh ee bah-gah-lyee) – *Where can I collect my luggage?*
Essential for when you've just landed and are ready to start your adventure.

Navigating the airport can be a breeze when you know what to say. Plus, starting your trip with a few Italian phrases will get you in the spirit of adventure right from the get-go!

With these travel and transportation phrases in your pocket, you'll move through Italy with confidence and ease. From catching a bus to renting a car, you're ready to explore everything this beautiful country has to offer. Buon viaggio e buon divertimento! (Have a great trip and lots of fun!)

CHAPTER 3

Accomodation

F inding the perfect place to stay is a key part of any trip, and in Italy, it's all about comfort, charm, and a touch of la dolce vita. Whether you're checking into a luxury hotel in Rome, a quaint B&B in Tuscany, or a cozy hostel in Florence, knowing the right phrases will make your stay much more enjoyable. In this section, we'll cover everything from booking your room to handling any little issues that might pop up—because even in paradise, sometimes you need an extra towel!

Checking into a Hotel

First impressions matter, and checking into your hotel with a bit of Italian will surely make a great one. Here's how to breeze through the check-in process and start your stay on the right foot.

- **Ho una prenotazione.** (oh oo-nah preh-noh-tah-tsee-oh-neh) – *I have a reservation.*
  Let the hotel staff know you've already booked your stay.
- **Il mio nome è...** (eel mee-oh noh-meh eh) – *My name is...*
  A simple way to introduce yourself when you're checking in.
- **Potrei avere la chiave, per favore?** (poh-trey ah-veh-reh lah kee-ah-veh, pehr fah-voh-reh) – *Could I have the key, please?*
  Asking for your room key with a smile.
- **A che ora è la colazione?** (ah keh oh-rah eh lah koh-lah-tsee-oh-neh) – *What time is breakfast?*
  Important to know when to enjoy that delicious Italian breakfast!
- **Dov'è l'ascensore?** (doh-veh lah-shen-soh-reh) – *Where is the elevator?*
  Handy for when you need to find your way to your room, especially if you're carrying heavy luggage.
- **Il Wi-Fi è gratuito?** (eel wee-fee eh grah-too-ee-toh) – *Is the Wi-Fi free?*
  Because staying connected is essential, even on vacation.

These phrases will help you glide through the check-in process, ensuring you start your stay smoothly and without any hiccups. Plus, a little Italian will make the staff smile and might even get you a few extra perks!

Booking and Inquiring About Rooms

Whether you're booking in advance or walking into a hotel on a whim, these phrases will help you secure the perfect room for your stay.

▶ **Vorrei prenotare una camera.** (vor-ray preh-noh-tah-reh oo-nah kah-meh-rah) – *I'd like to book a room.*
Great for when you're making a reservation ahead of time.

▶ **Avete camere disponibili?** (ah-veh-teh kah-meh-reh dee-spoh-nee-bee-lee) – *Do you have any rooms available?*
Use this when you're checking availability upon arrival.

▶ **Quanto costa per notte?** (kwan-toh koh-stah pehr noht-teh) – *How much is it per night?*
An important question for managing your budget.

▶ **Vorrei una camera con vista, per favore.** (vor-ray oo-nah kah-meh-rah kohn vee-stah, pehr fah-voh-reh) – *I'd like a room with a view, please.*
Because who doesn't want to wake up to a stunning Italian vista?

▶ **C'è l'aria condizionata?** (cheh lah-ree-ah kohn-dee-tsyoh-nah-tah) – *Is there air conditioning?*
A must-know during the warm Italian summers.

▶ **La colazione è inclusa?** (lah koh-lah-tsee-oh-neh eh een-kloo-zah) – *Is breakfast included?*
Make sure you know what's covered before you settle in.

With these phrases, you can confidently book your accommodation and ensure all your needs are met, leaving you free to enjoy your stay without any surprises.

Dealing with Issues
(e.g., Asking for Extra Towels, Reporting Problems)

Even in the most charming of hotels, little issues can arise. But don't worry—with these phrases, you'll be able to handle any situation with ease and keep your stay as relaxing as possible.

▶ **Potrei avere degli asciugamani extra, per favore?** (poh-trey ah-veh-reh deh-lyee ah-shoo-gah-mah-nee eks-trah, pehr fah-voh-reh) – *Could I have some extra towels, please?*
Perfect for when you need a bit more comfort.

▶ **C'è un problema con...** (cheh oon proh-bleh-mah kohn...) – *There's a problem with...*
Use this phrase to address any issues, like: *C'è un problema con l'aria condizionata* (There's a problem with the air conditioning).

▶ **La doccia non funziona.** (lah doh-chah nohn foon-tsee-oh-nah) – *The shower isn't working.*
A straightforward way to report a common issue.

▶ **Potrebbe aiutarmi, per favore?** (poh-trehb-beh ah-yoo-tar-mee pehr fah-voh-reh) – *Could you help me, please?*
When you need assistance with something in your room or around the hotel.

▶ **Quando sarà risolto il problema?** (kwan-doh sah-rah ree-sohl-toh eel proh-bleh-mah) – *When will the problem be fixed?*
A polite way to ask when you can expect an issue to be resolved.

These phrases will help you handle any small hiccups during your stay without stress. With a polite request and a friendly attitude, most issues will be resolved quickly, allowing you to get back to enjoying your Italian getaway.

With these accommodation phrases in your toolkit, you'll be ready to check in, settle in, and handle any situation like a seasoned traveler. Your stay in Italy is sure to be comfortable, memorable, and most importantly—stress-free! Buon soggiorno! (Enjoy your stay!)

CHAPTER 4
Eating Out

Eating in Italy is not just about filling your stomach—it's a whole experience, a celebration of food, culture, and life itself. From savoring a simple pizza in a local trattoria to enjoying a multi-course meal in a fancy ristorante, dining out in Italy is a delight for the senses. Knowing a few key phrases will help you navigate menus, order like a pro, and enjoy every bite of your culinary adventure. Let's dig in!

Ordering at a Restaurant

Ordering food in Italy is an exciting moment. With these phrases, you can confidently ask for what you want and maybe even try something new!

- **Vorrei ordinare, per favore.** (vor-ray or-dee-nah-reh, pehr fah-voh-reh) – *I'd like to order, please.*
  This is your go-to phrase when you're ready to let the server know what you want.
- **Cosa mi consiglia?** (koh-zah mee kohn-seel-yah) – *What do you recommend?*
  Perfect for when you're feeling adventurous and want to try something special.
- **Prendo...** (pren-doh) – *I'll have...*
  Use this to state your choice: *Prendo una pizza margherita* (I'll have a margherita pizza).
- **Un bicchiere di vino rosso, per favore.** (oon beek-kyer-reh dee vee-noh roh-soh, pehr fah-voh-reh) – *A glass of red wine, please.*
  Wine is a must-try in Italy, and this phrase will help you order it with ease.
- **Posso avere un menu, per favore?** (pohs-soh ah-veh-reh oon meh-noo, pehr fah-voh-reh) – *Can I have a menu, please?*
  Ask for the menu when you're ready to make your selection.
- **Vorrei un bicchiere d'acqua, per favore.** (vor-ray oon beek-kyer-reh dah-kwah, pehr fah-voh-reh) – *I'd like a glass of water, please.*
  If you prefer water over wine, this will come in handy.

Ordering your meal in Italian not only helps you get exactly what you want but also adds to the authentic experience. Plus, the staff will appreciate your effort to speak their language!

Understanding the Menu

Italian menus are filled with delicious options, but they can be a bit overwhelming if you're not familiar with the language. Here's how to navigate them with confidence.

▶ **Antipasto** (ahn-tee-pah-stoh) – *Appetizer*
Start your meal off with something light and delicious, like bruschetta or prosciutto.

▶ **Primo** (pree-moh) – *First course*
Usually a pasta or risotto dish. Italians take their first courses seriously!

▶ **Secondo** (seh-kohn-doh) – *Second course*
This is the main dish, often meat or fish. Pair it with a side dish (contorno).

▶ **Dolce** (dohl-cheh) – *Dessert*
Save room for dessert—whether it's gelato, tiramisu, or panna cotta, you're in for a treat.

▶ **C'è qualcosa senza glutine?** (cheh kwahl-koh-sah sen-tzah gloot-ee-neh) – *Is there anything gluten-free?*
Essential for those with gluten sensitivities.

▶ **Vegetariano** (veh-jeh-tah-ree-ah-noh) – *Vegetarian*
Look for this word if you're avoiding meat.

▶ **Allergico/a a...** (ahl-lehr-jee-koh/kah ah) – *Allergic to...*
Fill in the blank with what you need to avoid, like *Allergico/a alle noci* (Allergic to nuts).

▶ **Il piatto del giorno** (eel pee-aht-toh del jor-noh) – *The dish of the day*
Always ask about this—restaurants often have daily specials that are worth trying.

With these menu basics, you'll be able to navigate your options and choose dishes that suit your taste and dietary needs. Remember, trying new things is part of the fun!

Dietary Preferences and Allergies

If you have specific dietary needs, it's important to communicate them clearly. These phrases will help you enjoy your meal without worry.

- **Sono vegetariano/a.** (soh-noh veh-jeh-tah-ree-ah-noh/nah) – *I'm vegetarian.*
  Use this to let the server know you don't eat meat.
- **Sono vegano/a.** (soh-noh veh-gah-noh/nah) – *I'm vegan.*
  For those who avoid all animal products, this phrase is essential.
- **Non posso mangiare...** (nohn pohs-soh mahn-jah-reh) – *I can't eat...*
  Insert whatever you need to avoid: *Non posso mangiare latticini* (I can't eat dairy).
- **Ho un'allergia a...** (oh oon ahl-lehr-jee-ah ah) – *I have an allergy to...*
  Be specific to ensure the kitchen can accommodate your needs.
- **C'è qualcosa senza latticini?** (cheh kwahl-koh-sah sen-tzah laht-tee-chee-nee) – *Is there anything dairy-free?*
  Handy for those who need to avoid dairy products.
- **Può prepararlo senza...?** (pwoh preh-pah-rar-loh sen-tzah) – *Can you prepare it without...?*
  If a dish usually includes something you can't eat, ask if it can be made without it.

These phrases will help you communicate your dietary preferences and allergies, ensuring you can relax and enjoy your meal without any concerns.

Paying the Bill

Once you've enjoyed your delicious Italian meal, it's time to settle the bill. Here's how to do it smoothly and politely.

- **Il conto, per favore.** (eel kohn-toh, pehr fah-voh-reh) – *The bill, please.*
  A simple, straightforward way to ask for the check.
- **Posso pagare con carta?** (pohs-soh pah-gah-reh kohn kar-tah) – *Can I pay with a card?*
  Useful to know whether the restaurant accepts credit or debit cards.
- **Accettate carte di credito?** (ah-cheht-tah-teh kar-teh dee kreh-dee-toh) – *Do you accept credit cards?*
  Double-check if you're unsure about their payment options.
- **È incluso il servizio?** (eh een-kloo-soh eel sehr-veet-see-oh) – *Is the service included?*
  This helps you know if a tip is expected, as in some places the service charge is already added to the bill.
- **Ho solo contanti.** (oh soh-loh kohn-tahn-tee) – *I only have cash.*
  In case you're paying in cash and want to clarify this upfront.
- **Tenga il resto.** (tehn-gah eel reh-stoh) – *Keep the change.*
  A polite way to leave a tip if you're happy with the service.

Paying the bill in Italy is usually a relaxed affair—there's no rush, so take your time and enjoy the final moments of your dining experience. And don't forget to thank your server with a smile and a heartfelt *Grazie!*

With these phrases in your back pocket, you'll be able to dine out in Italy with ease, from ordering your meal to settling the bill. So go ahead, savor every bite, and enjoy the incredible flavors that Italy has to offer! Buon appetito!

CHAPTER 5

Shopping

Shopping in Italy is an adventure of its own! Whether you're browsing through high-end boutiques in Milan, haggling at a vibrant street market, or just picking up some essentials at the local supermarket, knowing a few key phrases will make the experience more enjoyable and maybe even help you score a better deal.

Common Shopping Phrases

Navigating shops in Italy is easy when you know what to say. These phrases will help you ask for what you need, understand what's on offer, and make your shopping trip a breeze.

▸ **Posso aiutarti?** (pohs-soh ah-yoo-tar-tee) – *Can I help you?*
You might hear this as soon as you walk into a store. A simple "No, grazie" works if you're just browsing, or "Sì, sto cercando..." if you need something specific.

▸ **Sto solo guardando, grazie.** (stoh soh-loh gwar-dan-doh, grah-tsyeh) – *I'm just looking, thank you.*
Perfect for when you want to browse without pressure.

▸ **Cercavo...** (cher-kah-voh) – *I was looking for...*
Use this to specify what you're hunting down: *Cercavo una borsa* (I was looking for a bag).

▸ **Avete...** (ah-veh-teh) – *Do you have...*
A quick way to check if the store has what you need: *Avete delle scarpe nere?* (Do you have black shoes?)

▸ **Dov'è il camerino?** (doh-veh eel kah-meh-ree-noh) – *Where is the fitting room?*
When you're ready to try on that perfect outfit.

▸ **Mi piace!** (mee pya-chay) – *I like it!*
Use this to express your approval if you find something you love.

▸ **Posso pagare con carta?** (pohs-soh pah-gah-reh kohn kar-tah) – *Can I pay with a card?*
Handy to know when you're ready to check out.

With these phrases, you'll feel confident walking into any shop in Italy, knowing you can communicate exactly what you need—or just enjoy browsing to your heart's content.

Asking for Prices and Bargaining

Shopping in Italy isn't just about picking up items—it's often about the experience, which might include a bit of bargaining, especially in markets. Here's how to ask about prices and maybe even negotiate a better deal.

▸ **Quanto costa?** (kwan-toh koh-stah) – *How much does it cost?*
The classic phrase to find out the price of an item.

▸ **È troppo caro.** (eh troh-poh kah-roh) – *It's too expensive.*
A polite way to express that the price is a bit out of your range, potentially opening the door for negotiation.

▸ **C'è uno sconto?** (cheh oo-noh skohn-toh) – *Is there a discount?*
Don't be shy to ask—sometimes you'll be pleasantly surprised!

▸ **Posso avere uno sconto?** (pohs-soh ah-veh-reh oo-noh skohn-toh) – *Can I have a discount?*
Direct, but polite—perfect for bargaining at markets or small shops.

▸ **Accettate carte di credito?** (ah-chet-tah-teh kar-teh dee kreh-dee-toh) – *Do you accept credit cards?*
Important to know before you commit to a purchase, especially if you're running low on cash.

▸ **Va bene, lo prendo.** (vah beh-neh, loh pren-doh) – *Okay, I'll take it.*
Seal the deal with this phrase once you're satisfied with the price.

Bargaining is part of the fun in Italian markets, so don't hesitate to engage with vendors—they often expect it and enjoy the interaction. Just keep it friendly and light-hearted!

Buying Essentials

(Supermarkets, Pharmacies)

Even when shopping for everyday essentials, it's helpful to know a few phrases. Whether you're grabbing snacks for a picnic or picking up some sunscreen, these phrases will make your shopping trip smooth and stress-free.

▸ **Dove posso trovare...?** (doh-veh pohs-soh troh-vah-rch) – *Where can I find...?*
Use this to ask for specific items: *Dove posso trovare l'acqua?* (Where can I find water?)

▸ **Ho bisogno di...** (oh bee-soh-nyoh dee) – *I need...*
Perfect for when you're looking for something specific: *Ho bisogno di un dentifricio* (I need toothpaste).

▸ **C'è una farmacia qui vicino?** (cheh oo-nah fahr-mah-chee-ah kwee vee-chee-noh) – *Is there a pharmacy nearby?*
Essential if you need any medical supplies or over-the-counter medications.

▸ **Posso avere una busta, per favore?** (pohs-soh ah-veh-reh oo-nah boos-tah, pehr fah-voh-reh) – *Can I have a bag, please?*
Useful when you're at the checkout and need something to carry your items.

▸ **Quanto costa questa?** (kwan-toh koh-stah kwes-tah) – *How much does this cost?*
Use this to check the price of an item if it's not labeled.

▸ **Mi serve qualcosa per il mal di testa.** (mee sehr-veh kwahl-koh-sah pehr eel mahl dee teh-stah) – *I need something for a headache.*
Handy in a pharmacy when you're not sure what to ask for.

Shopping for essentials might seem mundane, but with the right phrases, it becomes another opportunity to engage with the local culture. Plus, you'll never be at a loss when you need something quickly!

CHAPTER 6

Sightseeing and Activities

Italy is a treasure trove of incredible sights, from ancient ruins and stunning art galleries to breathtaking natural landscapes. Whether you're exploring the Colosseum, wandering through the Uffizi Gallery, or hiking in the Dolomites, knowing a few key phrases will help you make the most of your adventures.

Visiting Tourist Attractions

Exploring Italy's famous landmarks is a must, and these phrases will help you get the most out of your visits.

▶ **Dov'è l'ingresso?** (doh-veh leen-greh-soh) – *Where is the entrance?*
Use this to find your way into the attraction.

▶ **A che ora apre/chiude?** (ah keh oh-rah ah-preh/kew-deh) – *What time does it open/close?*
Essential for planning your visit to avoid any surprises.

▶ **C'è una guida in inglese?** (cheh oo-nah gwee-dah een een-gleh-zeh) – *Is there an English guide?*
Perfect for when you want to understand more about what you're seeing.

▶ **Dove sono i bagni?** (doh-veh soh-noh ee bahn-yee) – *Where are the bathrooms?*
Always a useful phrase, especially in large tourist spots.

▶ **Si può fare delle foto qui?** (see pwoh fah-reh deh-leh foh-toh kwee) – *Can you take photos here?*
Good to know before snapping pictures in museums or historical sites.

▶ **Quanto tempo ci vuole per visitarlo?** (kwan-toh tehm-poh chee vwaw-leh pehr vee-zee-tar-loh) – *How long does it take to visit?*
Helps you manage your schedule, especially if you have other plans for the day.

These phrases will ensure that your sightseeing experiences go smoothly, letting you focus on enjoying the beauty and history that Italy has to offer.

Booking Tours and Tickets

Italy is full of tours and special experiences, from guided walks through ancient ruins to wine tastings in the countryside. Here's how to book your spot and make sure everything goes according to plan.

▸ **Vorrei prenotare un tour.** (vor-ray preh-noh-tah-reh oon toor) – *I'd like to book a tour.*
Start off by letting the booking agent know what you want.

▸ **Quanto costa il biglietto?** (kwan-toh koh-stah eel beel-lyet-toh) – *How much does the ticket cost?*
Always good to know before you commit!

▸ **C'è uno sconto per studenti/senior?** (cheh oo-noh skohn-toh pehr stoo-den-tee/seh-nyor) – *Is there a discount for students/seniors?*
Handy if you're eligible for a discount.

▸ **È necessario prenotare in anticipo?** (eh neh-cheh-sahr-yoh preh-noh-tah-reh een ahn-tee-poh) – *Is it necessary to book in advance?*
Important to avoid disappointment, especially for popular attractions.

▸ **Dove posso comprare i biglietti?** (doh-veh pohs-soh kohm-prah-reh ee beel-lyet-tee) – *Where can I buy tickets?*
Use this to find the nearest ticket office or kiosk.

▸ **Posso pagare online?** (pohs-soh pah-gah-reh on-line) – *Can I pay online?*
Useful if you want to book your tickets ahead of time.

Booking tours and tickets in Italy is often straightforward, but these phrases will ensure you get exactly what you need without any hassle. Whether you're planning a guided tour of Pompeii or reserving a spot for a gondola ride in Venice, you'll be all set.

Describing Preferences

(e.g., Art, History, Nature)

Italy has something for everyone—whether you're an art lover, a history buff, or a nature enthusiast. Use these phrases to express your interests and get recommendations tailored to your preferences.

▸ **Mi piace l'arte.** (mee pya-chay l'ar-teh) – *I like art.*
Perfect for when you're looking to explore museums and galleries.

▸ **Sono interessato/a alla storia.** (soh-noh een-teh-rehs-sah-toh/ah ahl-lah stoh-ree-ah) – *I'm interested in history.*
Great for finding tours and sites that delve into Italy's rich past.

▸ **Preferisco la natura.** (preh-feh-ree-skoh lah nah-too-rah) – *I prefer nature.*
Use this when looking for outdoor activities, such as hikes or garden visits.

▸ **C'è qualcosa di interessante per i bambini?** (cheh kwahl-koh-sah dee een-teh-rehs-sahn-teh pehr ee bahm-bee-nee) – *Is there anything interesting for children?*
Handy for families traveling with kids who want to find something fun for the little ones.

▸ **Mi piace la fotografia.** (mee pya-chay lah fo-toh-grah-fee-ah) – *I like photography.*
This can lead to suggestions for the most photogenic spots.

▸ **Cerco qualcosa di fuori dai soliti percorsi turistici.** (cher-koh kwahl-koh-sah dee foo-oh-ree dai soh-lee-tee pehr-kor-see too-ree-stee-chee) – *I'm looking for something off the beaten path.*
Use this to discover hidden gems that are less crowded.

These phrases will help you tailor your Italian adventure to your own tastes, ensuring you spend your time on activities that truly interest you.

Taking Photos

Capturing memories is a big part of traveling, and Italy offers countless photo opportunities. Here's how to make sure you can take the perfect shot and even get in a few photos yourself!

- **Puoi scattarmi una foto, per favore?** (pwoh-ee skaht-tar-mee oo-nah foh-toh pehr fah-voh-reh) – *Can you take a picture of me, please?*
  Great for when you want a photo of yourself in front of the Trevi Fountain or the Leaning Tower of Pisa.

- **Dove posso trovare una buona inquadratura?** (doh-veh pohs-soh troh-vah-reh oo-nah bwoh-nah een-kwah-drah-too-rah) – *Where can I find a good view/angle?*
  Perfect for photographers looking for the best spot to capture that iconic image.

- **Posso fare una foto qui?** (pohs-soh fah-reh oo-nah foh-toh kwee) – *Can I take a photo here?*
  Always good to ask, especially in museums or churches where photography might be restricted.

- **C'è abbastanza luce?** (cheh ahb-bah-stahn-zah loo-cheh) – *Is there enough light?*
  Useful when you're trying to take a picture in dimly lit areas.

- **Potresti spostarti un po', per favore?** (poh-treh-stee spoh-star-tee oon poh, pehr fah-voh-reh) – *Could you move a little, please?*
  If someone is accidentally blocking your perfect shot, this phrase will help you out politely.

- **Mi puoi mandare la foto?** (mee pwoh-ee mahn-dah-reh lah foh-toh) – *Can you send me the photo?*
  If you've asked someone else to take a picture and you want a copy.

Taking photos is a wonderful way to remember your trip, and with these phrases, you'll be able to do so smoothly. Just don't forget to put the camera down every once in a while and soak in the beauty of Italy with your own eyes!

CHAPTER 7

Socializing

One of the best parts of traveling is meeting new people and immersing yourself in the local culture. In Italy, socializing is an art form, whether it's making new friends at a café, chatting with locals at a piazza, or understanding the nuances of Italian customs.

Meeting People

Making connections with locals or fellow travelers can make your trip even more memorable. These phrases will help you break the ice and start new friendships.

- **Ciao, mi chiamo...** (chow, mee kyah-moh) – *Hi, my name is...*
  A simple and friendly way to introduce yourself.
- **Piacere di conoscerti!** (pya-cheh-reh dee koh-noh-sher-tee) – *Nice to meet you!*
  This phrase will be your go-to after introductions, showing your enthusiasm to make new friends.
- **Di dove sei?** (dee doh-veh seh-ee) – *Where are you from?*
  A great conversation starter to learn more about the person you're speaking with.
- **Quanti anni hai?** (kwahn-tee ahn-nee ah-ee) – *How old are you?*
  Use this only if it feels appropriate—Italians can be quite open, but always read the situation!
- **Sei qui in vacanza?** (seh-ee kwee een vah-kahn-tsah) – *Are you here on vacation?*
  Perfect for meeting fellow travelers.
- **Lavori o studi?** (lah-voh-ree oh stoo-dee) – *Do you work or study?*
  A casual question that can lead to more in-depth conversations.
- **Ti va di prendere un caffè insieme?** (tee vah dee pren-deh-reh oon kah-feh een-syeh-meh) – *Would you like to grab a coffee together?*
  Coffee is a big part of social life in Italy, and this is a great way to extend a friendly meeting.

Meeting new people in Italy is usually easy and fun, thanks to the locals' warm and welcoming nature. These phrases will help you connect with others and maybe even make some lifelong friends!

Making Small Talk

Small talk is a great way to fill in the gaps and keep conversations flowing. Whether you're waiting for your pasta to arrive or just passing the time, these phrases will help you chat like a local.

- **Che tempo fa?** (keh tehm-poh fah) – *What's the weather like?*
  A classic and easy way to start a conversation.
- **Ti piace l'Italia?** (tee pya-cheh lee-tah-lyah) – *Do you like Italy?*
  This can lead to discussions about favorite places, experiences, and more.
- **Hai fratelli o sorelle?** (ah-ee frah-tehl-lee oh soh-rel-leh) – *Do you have brothers or sisters?*
  Family is important in Italy, and asking about it shows genuine interest.
- **Qual è il tuo piatto italiano preferito?** (kwahl eh eel too-oh pyah-toh ee-tah-lyah-noh preh-feh-ree-toh) – *What's your favorite Italian dish?*
  Food is always a safe and enjoyable topic of conversation in Italy!
- **Sei mai stato/a qui prima?** (seh-ee mah-ee stah-toh/ah kwee pree-mah) – *Have you been here before?*
  Perfect for learning about the other person's experiences in the area.
- **Che cosa fai nel tempo libero?** (keh koh-zah fah-ee nehl tehm-poh lee-beh-roh) – *What do you do in your free time?*
  A nice way to learn more about the person's hobbies and interests.

Small talk is a fun and relaxed way to get to know people better. Italians love to chat, so don't be afraid to dive into these conversations—they'll appreciate your effort!

Italian Etiquette and Customs

Understanding and respecting local customs is key to making a great impression in Italy. Here are some phrases and tips that will help you navigate social situations with grace.

- **Grazie mille!** (grah-tsyeh meel-leh) – *Thank you very much!*
  Italians value politeness, and a sincere thank you goes a long way.
- **Per favore** (pehr fah-voh-reh) – *Please*
  Always include this when making a request—it's the magic word in any language!
- **Mi scusi** (mee skoo-zee) – *Excuse me*
  Use this when you need to get someone's attention or apologize for a small mistake.
- **Prego!** (preh-goh) – *You're welcome!*
  A common response to "Grazie," it shows your good manners.
- **Buon appetito!** (bwohn ahp-peh-tee-toh) – *Enjoy your meal!*
  A polite and friendly thing to say before you and your companions start eating.
- **Baci sulla guancia** (bah-chee soo-lah gwahn-chah) – *Kisses on the cheek*
  Italians often greet close friends and family with a kiss on each cheek. Be ready for this warm greeting, but follow the lead of the person you're greeting—don't initiate unless they do!
- **Non si preoccupi.** (nohn see preh-oh-kkoo-pee) – *Don't worry.*
  Italians tend to be relaxed and don't sweat the small stuff. This phrase reflects that easy-going attitude.

Understanding these simple customs and using the right phrases will help you fit in and be seen as a respectful and polite visitor. Italians appreciate when you make an effort to understand and respect their way of life.

CHAPTER 8

Romance

Ah, Italy—the land of love, where romance seems to linger in the air! Whether you're swept off your feet by the beauty of the landscape or by a charming local, knowing a few romantic phrases can add a little extra magic to your Italian adventure.

Flirting and Compliments

Flirting in Italy is often light-hearted and full of charm. Here are some phrases to help you compliment someone or strike up a romantic conversation.

▸ **Sei bellissimo/a.** (seh-ee behl-lees-see-moh/mah) – *You are very handsome/beautiful.*
A classic compliment that's sure to make someone smile.

▸ **Hai un sorriso stupendo.** (ah-ee oon soh-ree-zoh stoo-pehn-doh) – *You have a wonderful smile.*
Perfect for complimenting that dazzling grin.

▸ **Ti trovo molto affascinante.** (tee troh-voh mohl-toh ah-fah-shee-nahn-teh) – *I find you very charming.*
A lovely way to let someone know you're interested.

▸ **Possiamo conoscerci meglio?** (pohs-see-ah-moh koh-noh-sher-chee meh-lyoh) – *Can we get to know each other better?*
Great for taking the conversation to the next level.

▸ **Hai degli occhi bellissimi.** (ah-ee deh-lyee ohk-kee behl-lees-see-mee) – *You have beautiful eyes.*
Another classic compliment that never fails to impress.

▸ **Ti va di fare una passeggiata?** (tee vah dee fah-reh oo-nah pahs-sej-jah-tah) – *Would you like to go for a walk?*
Suggesting a walk is a romantic way to spend more time together in Italy's beautiful settings.

Flirting in Italy is often playful and sincere, so don't be afraid to use these phrases to show your admiration. Just remember to keep it light and fun!

Expressing Affection

When the connection deepens and you want to express your feelings, these phrases will help you share what's in your heart.

- **Ti voglio bene.** (tee voh-lyoh beh-neh) – *I care about you.*
  A phrase used to express deep affection, often used among close friends or in a romantic context.
- **Sono innamorato/a di te.** (soh-noh een-nah-moh-rah-toh/ah dee teh) – *I'm in love with you.*
  When things get serious, this is how to let someone know you're in love.
- **Mi manchi.** (mee mahn-kee) – *I miss you.*
  Simple and heartfelt, perfect for when you're apart from someone special.
- **Non riesco a smettere di pensarti.** (nohn ree-ehs-koh ah smet-teh-reh dee pen-sar-tee) – *I can't stop thinking about you.*
  A phrase that shows someone is on your mind constantly.
- **Voglio stare con te.** (voh-lyoh stah-reh kohn teh) – *I want to be with you.*
  Direct and meaningful, this phrase leaves no doubt about your feelings.
- **Sei tutto/a per me.** (seh-ee toot-toh/ah pehr meh) – *You are everything to me.*
  A deeply romantic expression of affection.

These phrases can help you express your emotions in a way that's both sincere and romantic. Whether it's a budding romance or a deeper relationship, they'll help you communicate your feelings clearly.

Discussing Relationships

As your relationship develops, you might want to have deeper conversations about where things are heading. Here are some phrases to help you navigate those discussions.

- **Cosa pensi di noi?** (koh-zah pen-see dee noh-ee) – *What do you think about us?*
  A good way to start a conversation about your relationship status.
- **Cosa cerchi in una relazione?** (koh-zah cher-kee een oo-nah reh-lah-tsee-oh-neh) – *What are you looking for in a relationship?*
  Perfect for understanding each other's intentions and expectations.
- **Ti vedi con qualcun altro/a?** (tee veh-dee kohn kwahl-koon ahl-troh/ah) – *Are you seeing someone else?*
  A delicate but sometimes necessary question in new relationships.
- **Vorrei che fossimo esclusivi.** (vor-ray keh fohs-see-moh ehk-skloo-see-vee) – *I'd like us to be exclusive.*
  When you're ready to take things to the next level.
- **Dove pensi che andremo a finire?** (doh-veh pen-see keh ahn-dreh-moh ah fee-nee-reh) – *Where do you think this is going?*
  A thoughtful question for discussing the future of your relationship.
- **Vorrei passare più tempo con te.** (vor-ray pahs-sah-reh pyoo tehm-poh kohn teh) – *I'd like to spend more time with you.*
  This phrase shows your desire to deepen the relationship.

Discussing relationships can be challenging, but with these phrases, you'll be able to communicate your thoughts and feelings clearly and respectfully. Remember, honesty and openness are key in any relationship, and these phrases will help you express yourself in a thoughtful and caring way.

CHAPTER 9

Emergencies

While we hope your trip to Italy is smooth and carefree, it's always wise to be prepared for the unexpected. Whether you're dealing with a medical issue, reporting a theft, or simply need to contact the local authorities, knowing the right phrases can make a stressful situation much easier to handle.

Medical Emergencies

If you find yourself needing medical assistance, these phrases will help you communicate effectively with healthcare providers and ensure you receive the care you need.

- **Ho bisogno di un medico.** (oh bee-zoh-nyoh dee oon meh-dee-koh) – *I need a doctor.*
  Use this when you need to see a doctor urgently.
- **Mi sento male.** (mee sen-toh mah-leh) – *I feel sick.*
  A general phrase to describe feeling unwell.
- **Mi fa male qui.** (mee fah mah-leh kwee) – *It hurts here.*
  Useful for pointing out where you're experiencing pain.
- **Ho un'allergia a...** (oh oon ahl-lehr-jee-ah ah) – *I have an allergy to...*
  Important for letting medical staff know about any allergies, such as *Ho un'allergia alla penicillina* (I have an allergy to penicillin).
- **C'è un ospedale qui vicino?** (cheh oon ohs-peh-dah-leh kwee vee-chee-noh) – *Is there a hospital nearby?*
  Essential for finding the nearest hospital.
- **Mi sono fatto/a male.** (mee soh-noh faht-toh/ah mah-leh) – *I hurt myself.*
  Use this to describe an injury you've sustained.
- **Ho bisogno di un'ambulanza.** (oh bee-zoh-nyoh dee oon ahm-boo-lahn-tsah) – *I need an ambulance.*
  In case of a severe emergency, this phrase will help you get immediate assistance.

Knowing these phrases can make a significant difference in a medical emergency, helping you get the right treatment quickly. Remember, in Italy, the emergency number for medical help is **118**.

Reporting a Crime or Theft

If you become a victim of a crime or theft, it's important to report it to the authorities. These phrases will help you explain the situation and get the assistance you need.

- **Mi hanno rubato...** (mee ahn-noh roo-bah-toh) – *I've been robbed of...*
  Use this to describe what was stolen: *Mi hanno rubato il portafoglio* (They stole my wallet).
- **Ho bisogno di aiuto.** (oh bee-zoh-nyoh dee ah-yoo-toh) – *I need help.*
  A general phrase to ask for assistance in any emergency.
- **Dov'è la stazione di polizia?** (doh-veh lah stah-tsee-oh-neh dee poh-lee-tsee-ah) – *Where is the police station?*
  Important for finding where to report a crime.
- **Voglio denunciare un furto.** (vohl-lyoh deh-noon-chah-reh oon fohr-toh) – *I want to report a theft.*
  Use this to formally report a theft to the police.
- **Qualcuno mi ha aggredito.** (kwahl-koo-noh mee ah ahg-greh-dee-toh) – *Someone assaulted me.*
  Important for reporting an assault.
- **Posso fare una dichiarazione?** (pohs-soh fah-reh oo-nah dee-kya-rah-tsee-oh-neh) – *Can I make a statement?*
  Use this when you need to provide a statement about the incident.
- **C'è un testimone?** (cheh oon tehs-tee-moh-neh) – *Is there a witness?*
  Helpful to ask if anyone saw the incident and can corroborate your story.

Reporting a crime can be stressful, but these phrases will help you communicate effectively with the police and ensure that the incident is properly recorded and handled. The emergency number for police in Italy is **112**.

Important Contact Numbers

(Police, Ambulance, Embassy)

In an emergency, knowing the right contact numbers can be a lifesaver. Here's a list of important numbers to keep handy while traveling in Italy:

- **Polizia di Stato (State Police): 113**
  For reporting accidents, theft, or any situation requiring police assistance.
- **Ambulanza (Ambulance/Medical Emergency Service): 118**
  For medical emergencies, including mountain or cave rescue. This number connects you to emergency medical services.
- **Vigili del Fuoco (Fire Department): 115**
  For fire emergencies or weather-related emergencies.
- **Soccorso Stradale (Roadside Assistance): 803.116**
  This number connects you to the Automobile Club d'Italia (ACI) for emergency roadside assistance, available 24/7.
- **Guardia Forestale (Forest Rangers): 1515**
  For emergencies related to forests, wildlife, or environmental protection.
- **Viaggiare Informati (Travel Information): 1518**
  This number provides travel information, including road conditions and traffic updates.
- **Soccorso in Mare (Sea Rescue): 1530**
  For emergencies at sea, this number will connect you to the coast guard.
- **Numero di Emergenza (General Emergency Number): 112**
  The European-wide emergency number, which connects you to the appropriate service, whether you need police, fire, or medical assistance.
- **Ambasciata degli Stati Uniti a Roma (U.S. Embassy in Rome):** +39 06 46741
  For U.S. citizens needing assistance from the American Embassy.
- **Ambasciata Britannica a Roma (British Embassy in Rome):** +39 06 4220 0001
  For British citizens needing assistance from the British Embassy.

These numbers are essential for ensuring your safety and getting the help you need as quickly as possible. It's a good idea to save these contacts on your phone and keep a written copy with you, just in case.

CHAPTER 10

Italian Slang for Everyday Conversations

I f you really want to sound like a local, learning a bit of
Italian slang is the way to go! Slang adds flavor to your
conversations, helping you fit in and understand the locals
on a whole new level. Plus, it's just plain fun! Whether
you're hanging out with friends, making small talk, or just
trying to sound less like a tourist, these phrases will give
your Italian a playful twist.

Understanding Common Italian Slang

Slang is all about being in the know. Here are some popular Italian slang expressions that you'll hear in everyday conversations, and which will make you sound like you've been living in Italy for years!

- **Che figata!** (keh fee-gah-tah) – *How cool!*
  Use this to express excitement or approval when something impresses you.
- **Boh!** (boh) – *I don't know!*
  This is the perfect way to shrug off a question you're unsure about. It's the Italian equivalent of "meh" or "dunno."
- **Magari!** (mah-gah-ree) – *I wish!*
  This phrase expresses hope or wishful thinking, often used when you really want something to happen.
- **Figo/Figa** (fee-goh/fee-gah) – *Cool/Hot*
  Use this to describe someone or something that's attractive or impressive. Be careful with "figa," though—it can be a bit more informal!
- **Tipo** (tee-poh) – *Dude/Guy*
  A casual way to refer to a guy, similar to "dude" in English. *Tipo* can also mean "kind of" or "like" in a filler-word sense.
- **Ci sta!** (chee stah) – *That works!*
  A flexible phrase that means something is good, acceptable, or just right. Use it when you agree with a suggestion.
- **Meno male!** (meh-noh mah-leh) – *Thank goodness!*
  A common phrase expressing relief, like when something bad is avoided.
- **Dai!** (dah-ee) – *Come on!*
  This versatile word can express encouragement, disbelief, or impatience, depending on your tone. It's a staple in Italian conversations.

These slang phrases are perfect for everyday use and will help you blend in with the locals, adding a dash of Italian flair to your speech. Just remember to use them in the right context to keep things light and fun!

Examples of Slang in Different Contexts

(Casual Greetings, Socializing, etc.)

Now that you've got the basics down, let's see how to use Italian slang in different social situations. Here are some examples of how to incorporate slang into your casual conversations.

Casual Greetings:

▸ **Ehi, come butta?** (eh-ee, koh-meh boot-tah) – *Hey, how's it going?*
A laid-back way to ask someone how they're doing.

▸ **Tutto a posto?** (toot-toh ah poh-stoh) – *Everything good?*
Use this to check in on a friend or see how things are going.

Socializing:

▸ **Ci facciamo una birra?** (chee fah-chah-mo oo-nah beer-rah) – *Shall we grab a beer?*
A friendly suggestion for hanging out over drinks.

▸ **Facciamo un giro?** (fah-chah-mo oon jee-roh) – *Shall we go for a walk/ drive?*
Perfect for suggesting a casual stroll or ride with friends.

Expressing Surprise or Disbelief:

▸ **Ma dai!** (mah dah-ee) – *No way!/Come on!*
Use this when you're surprised or skeptical about something someone said.

▸ **Che cavolo!** (keh kah-voh-loh) – *What the heck!*
A mild exclamation for when something unexpected or frustrating happens.

Agreeing with Someone:

▸ **Esatto!** (eh-zaht-toh) – *Exactly!*
Use this to show that you completely agree with what someone just said.

▸ **Ci sta, ci sta!** (chee stah, chee stah) – *That's right, that's right!*
An enthusiastic way to agree with a suggestion or statement.

Showing Excitement:

- **Spacca!** (spahk-kah) – *It rocks!/It's awesome!*
  Use this to express that something is really cool or impressive.
- **Che bomba!** (keh bom-bah) – *What a blast!*
  This is great for describing something super fun or exciting.

A Little Bit of the Naughty Stuff

No exploration of slang would be complete without touching on some of the more colorful expressions you might hear—or even want to use in the right context. Just remember, these phrases can be strong, so use them with care and only in the right company!

▸ **Cazzo!** (kaht-tsoh) – *Damn!/Shit!*
This is one of the most common expletives in Italian, used to express frustration or surprise. It's very informal, so be careful where and when you use it!

▸ **Che palle!** (keh pahl-leh) – *What a pain!/How annoying!*
Literally translating to "What balls!" this phrase is used to express annoyance or frustration with a situation.

▸ **Stronzo** (strohn-tsoh) – *Asshole*
A strong insult used to describe someone who's being particularly unpleasant. Definitely not something to say lightly!

▸ **Porca miseria!** (por-kah mee-zeh-ree-ah) – *Damn it!/For crying out loud!*
A milder expletive that's still expressive but less harsh than some of the others.

▸ **Vai a quel paese!** (vah-ee ah kwel pah-eh-zeh) – *Go to hell!*
A more polite way of telling someone off, literally translating to "Go to that village!"

▸ **Vaffanculo!** (vahf-fahn-koo-loh) – *Fuck off!*
A very strong and offensive expression, so use it sparingly and only if you're absolutely sure it's appropriate!

These phrases are a part of everyday language for many Italians, but they can be quite strong depending on the context and tone. If you decide to use them, make sure you're in the right setting and with people who won't take offense. And as always, keep it light and playful!

CHAPTER 11

Regional Italian Slang

Italy is a country rich in cultural diversity, and this is reflected in its language. Each region has its own unique slang and expressions that give a local flavor to the Italian spoken there. Whether you're in the bustling streets of Milan, the historic heart of Rome, or the sunny coasts of Naples, knowing a few regional phrases will help you connect with locals and show that you're more than just a tourist.

Key Phrases and Expressions by Region

(Northern, Central, Southern Italy)

Italy's regional differences are pronounced, especially when it comes to slang. Here are some key phrases from different parts of the country that will help you sound like a local wherever you go.

Northern Italy:

▸ **Milan: Bella lì!** (beh-lah lee) – *Hey there, good to see you!*
A casual greeting among friends in Milan, perfect for starting a conversation.

▸ **Turin: Bagnacauda** (bahn-yah-kow-dah) – *Warm dip*
While this refers to a traditional dish from the Piedmont region, it's often used to describe something comforting or welcoming.

▸ **Venice: Se magna?** (seh mah-nyah) – *Are we eating?*
In Venetian dialect, this is how you ask if it's time to eat, a crucial question in food-loving Italy!

Central Italy:

▸ **Rome: Annamo!** (ahn-nah-moh) – *Let's go!*
The Roman way of saying "andiamo." Use it to rally your friends or when you're ready to head out.

▸ **Florence: Ganzo!** (gahn-zoh) – *Cool!*
A Florentine slang word to express that something or someone is really cool or interesting.

▸ **Florence: Babbo** (bahb-boh) – *Dad*
In Florence, *babbo* means "dad," whereas in most other parts of Italy, *papà* is more common.

Southern Italy:

▸ **Naples: Ué!** (oo-eh) – *Hey!*
A typical Neapolitan greeting, often used to grab someone's attention or simply to say hello.

▸ **Sicily: Minchia!** (meen-kyah) – *Wow!/Damn!*
This is a very strong Sicilian exclamation used to express surprise or

frustration. Use it carefully!

- **Sicily: Camurria** (kah-moor-ree-ah) – *Annoyance/Nuisance*
  This Sicilian term is used to describe something or someone that's particularly annoying.

These phrases will help you blend in and show that you're attuned to the local way of speaking. Locals will appreciate your effort to use their regional slang!

Unique Regional Words and Their Meanings

Italy's regions not only have their own slang phrases but also unique words that don't exist elsewhere in the country. Here are some of the most interesting regional words and what they mean:

Northern Italy:

▶ **Tofeja** (toh-feh-yah) – *Clay pot*
In the Piedmont region, this word refers to a specific type of clay pot used in traditional cooking. It's often used to talk about hearty, home-cooked meals.

▶ **Ciapa** (chah-pah) – *Take*
In Lombardy, especially around Milan, "ciapa" is used instead of the standard Italian "prendi" (take).

Central Italy:

▶ **Bischero** (bees-keh-roh) – *Fool*
In Florence, this word is commonly used to affectionately call someone a fool or a joker.

▶ **Cencio** (chen-choh) – *Rag*
A Tuscan word for a rag or piece of cloth, but it's also used to describe something shabby or worn out.

Southern Italy:

▶ **Cafone** (kah-foh-neh) – *Rude person*
In the South, particularly in Campania, this word is used to describe someone who is uncouth or lacking in manners.

▶ **Sciroccato** (shee-roh-kah-toh) – *Crazy*
A Sicilian term often used to describe someone who's acting a bit wild or irrational, deriving from the hot "Scirocco" winds.

These unique words are great for adding local flavor to your Italian and showing that you understand the subtleties of regional dialects.

How to Adapt Your Italian
(Depending on the Region)

Italy's regions are so distinct that you may need to tweak your Italian depending on where you are. Here are some tips on how to adapt your language to fit in with the locals:

▶ **Observe and Listen:** The best way to adapt is to listen to how locals speak. Notice the words and expressions they use and try to incorporate them into your own speech. It's also a great way to pick up on the local accent!

▶ **Start Simple:** Begin with basic phrases and greetings, and then gradually incorporate more regional slang as you become more comfortable. For example, start with a simple "Ciao!" and then try out "Ué!" when you're in Naples.

▶ **Ask Locals for Help:** Don't be afraid to ask your new friends or acquaintances for tips on speaking like a local. Italians are usually happy to share their dialect and slang with you, and it can be a great conversation starter.

▶ **Be Flexible:** If you're traveling through multiple regions, be prepared to switch up your language. What works in Milan might not make sense in Naples, so stay adaptable and enjoy the diversity of the Italian language.

▶ **Use Humor:** Italians love a good joke, especially when it comes to language. Don't be afraid to laugh at yourself if you make a mistake—it's all part of the learning process, and it can help endear you to the locals.

By adapting your Italian to the region you're in, you'll not only enhance your communication skills but also show respect and appreciation for the local culture. Plus, it's a fun way to immerse yourself more deeply in the Italian experience!

Conclusion

As you wrap up your Italian adventure, it's time to reflect on all the incredible experiences you've had—and the new language skills you've picked up along the way. Whether you've been ordering gelato in perfect Italian, chatting with locals, or even picking up some regional slang, you've taken great steps towards connecting with Italy on a deeper level.

Additional Resources for Learning Italian

If you're excited to continue your Italian language journey, there are plenty of resources to help you dive deeper and keep improving your skills. Here are a few suggestions:

Language Learning Apps:

▸ **Duolingo**: A fun and interactive way to practice Italian daily with bite-sized lessons.

▸ **Babbel**: Offers structured courses that focus on conversational Italian and practical phrases.

▸ **Memrise**: Uses spaced repetition and real-life video clips to help you learn Italian in context.

Online Courses:

▸ **Coursera and edX**: Both offer comprehensive Italian language courses from universities around the world.

▸ **ItalianPod101**: Provides podcasts and video lessons for learners at all levels, focusing on practical language skills.

Italian Media:

▸ **Movies and TV Shows**: Watch Italian films or series with subtitles to improve your listening skills and pick up new phrases. Try classics like *La Dolce Vita* or modern hits like *Gomorra*.

▸ **Music**: Listen to Italian music to get a feel for the rhythm and melody of the language. Artists like Laura Pausini, Jovanotti, and Eros Ramazzotti are great starting points.

▸ **Books**: Start with dual-language books or children's books to build your reading skills. As you progress, try more challenging literature like the works of Italo Calvino or Elena Ferrante.

Language Exchange:

▸ **Tandem or HelloTalk**: These apps connect you with native Italian speakers who want to learn English, allowing you to practice speaking in a real-world context.

Travel Again:

▸ There's no better way to learn a language than by immersing yourself in the culture. If possible, plan another trip to Italy to continue practicing your Italian in the most authentic way possible.

Thank you for taking this linguistic journey with us! We hope this phrasebook has made your trip to Italy even more enjoyable and has sparked a love for the Italian language and culture. Remember, this is just the beginning—keep exploring, keep learning, and most importantly, keep having fun. Buona fortuna e buon viaggio! (Good luck and happy travels!)

Made in the USA
Las Vegas, NV
31 December 2024